Vanished Windsor

Compiled by Elias Kupfermann, MA, FRGS

Vanished Windsor

Compiled by
Elias Kupfermann, MA, FRGS

Windsor Local
History Group

Cover Illustration
The houses in Lower Thames Street, built in the Castle Ditch. Watercolour by John Preston Neale, 1846. Reproduced by kind permission of the Provost and Fellows of Eton College.

Back Cover Illustration
The west end of Windsor Castle from the Great Western Station, by George M. Henton, 1908.

The Windsor Local History Group was formed in 1976 from a small group of WEA students and tutors with the aim of fostering research in the field of local history and publishing the results.

Officers in 2010
Chair: Hester Davenport
Secretary: Sue Ashley
Treasurer: Barbara Mitch

First published 2010

Typeset by Thamesweb, Windsor

Cover design by Robert Brien, iModel Creative Media

Printed by Caric Press Ltd, Bournemouth, BH11 9UB

ISBN No. 0 9505 5677 7

Photographic Credits

Note: every effort has been made to credit sources of all illustrations in this book: if there are any errors or omissions please contact the Windsor Local History Group so corrections can be made in any subsequent editions.

The Royal Collection © 2010 Her Majesty Queen Elizabeth II: 5, 7-8,11, 48, 64, 71, 80-81, 93

Brigitte Mitchell – Private Collection: 50, 54, 136

Hendon Publishing : 15, 24, 33, 44, 73, 103, 106, 129, 135

Elias Kupfermann – Private Collection: 2-4, 6, 9, 12-13, 19, 23, 32, 41, 45, 55, 61, 65, 68-70, 82, 88, 89, 94, 98, 102, 114, 115, 132

Pamela Marson – Private Collection: 38

Royal Windsor Website.com: 14, 16, 31, 34, 62, 67, 90, 96, 99-100, 108, 111, 123, 124-5, 128, 138, 140

The Household Cavalry Museum: 137

The Record Office for Leicestershire, Leicester and Rutland: 17, 26, 29, 30, 51, 66, 92, 113

Geoffrey Try – Private Collection: 20-22, 25, 37, 39, 40, 43, 52-53, 57-59, 63, 74-77, 91, 97, 101, 104-5, 107, 120, 131, 133-134,139

Windsor and Royal Borough Museum: 10, 41, 42, 46, 60, 112

Windsor Express: 28, 47, 49, 83-84, 95, 97, 109-10, 116

Contents

The Colour Plates are included between pages 50 and 51

Peascod Street, William Street, Victoria Street & St Leonard's Road **76**

Index **97**

Foreword

There are two sides to the town of Windsor – one is the regal spectacle of pomp and circumstance which goes with all the trappings of a royal residence. The other, which is often seen as the poor relation, is the town of Windsor itself. On closer examination, however, both castle and town have been enriched not only by their architectural legacy but also by the customs and celebrations of their past inhabitants.

From medieval times both castle and town have adapted to change, be it a reaction to war or to peace, or the latest taste in fashion or architecture. With these changes, buildings or parts of buildings were demolished or remodelled either within the castle precincts or in the town itself and new buildings appeared. New fashions produced a myriad of new shops, goods and services and when these changed, businesses had to either adapt or simply vanish.

Using historic drawings, prints and paintings it is possible to chart the early development of the town of Windsor over several centuries. Ruling monarchs employed the best of artists, architects and craftsmen to work at the castle. These artists unwittingly recorded in their work glimpses of not only of life in the Royal palace but also in the bustling and thriving town below. The invention of the camera, in particular, produced a method of capturing events as they happened. This ensured they were then frozen in time. An accurate record of the past could be made to show scenes of a bygone age.

Vanished Windsor utilises a variety of pictorial sources to explore the ways in which both the castle and town have changed over the centuries from the earliest known prints and drawings to the 1970s. The idea for this book came about when I was asked to produce a talk on twentieth-century Windsor through old photos, which proved very popular. In the research for this talk it became apparent that many of Windsor's historic buildings had been demolished and little attempt had been made to record them graphically and to contextualise them in terms of their historical importance.

This book looks at the changing face of the very historic core of Windsor and can be viewed as a street by street pictorial record of central Windsor's both vanished and changing built heritage. Although there are many buildings which have changed or vanished throughout Windsor, due to size constraints this book geographically covers the main central medieval streets of Windsor and its later eighteenth century extensions.

Three main strands reverberate throughout this book; they are firstly buildings which have been destroyed over the centuries, scenes of social historical interest in the form of processions and celebrations and finally buildings which still exist today but have changed in some shape or form. These strands combine to make up the very essence of *Vanished Windsor*.

I should like to thank Her Majesty Queen Elizabeth II for access and gracious permission to reproduce several of the images. I am grateful to the Windsor Local History Group for their support and assistance in producing this publication, in particular Hester Davenport, Brigitte Mitchell and Roger Cullingham. The Royal Albert Institute Trust and the Prince Philip Trust have awarded generous loans towards publication costs. I should also like to record my gratitude to the Provost and Fellows of Eton College, the Cinema Theatre Association Archive, the Record Office for Leicestershire, Leicester and Rutland, the Windsor Express, the Windsor and Royal Borough Museum and The Royal Windsor Website for permission to reproduce many images from their extensive collections.

I am most grateful to Geoffrey Try for access to and use of his archive of historic Windsor and for the help of the Isaacs family. Thanks go to David Lewis for commenting on the draft and providing me with information about Windsor in the Medieval period. Alison Haymonds kindly provided me with information on Windsor's cinemas, and I should finally like to express my thanks to The Royal Windsor Website.com for their assistance and to John Handcock who had the foresight to record buildings which were demolished in the 1970s.

The Castle

1 North View of Windsor Castle with Eton College c.1445

This is the earliest known representation of Windsor Castle and shows the Castle after Edward III's great rebuilding programme which was begun almost a century earlier in 1350. A large courtyard is shown in the lower ward with a number of ancillary domestic buildings and the College of St George. St George's Chapel is yet to be built. This drawing is a later addition to Higden's *Polychronicon*, a universal world history, written in Latin and housed in Eton College Library. (MS213 – c.1420)

2 View of Windsor Castle from the North – Braun & Hogenberg – 1572

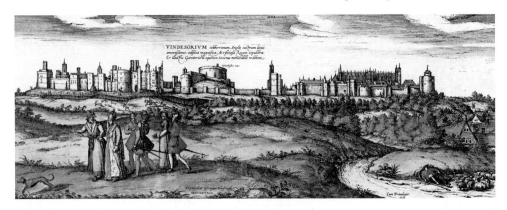

This view is the first image of Edward IV's St George's Chapel, often said to be the finest example of perpendicular gothic in the country, built from 1475. Also shown is the Norman motte and its round tower which dates from the late twelfth century. Note the defensive wall which cuts across the motte and formed the castle's middle ward.

3 Prospect of Windsor Castle from the North – Wenceslaus Hollar – 1667

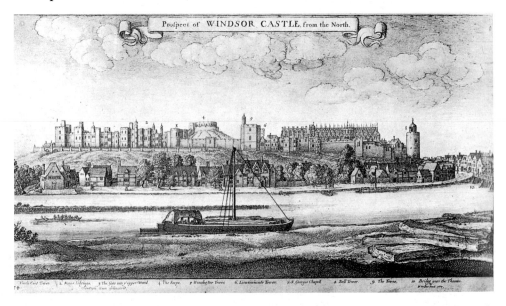

This etching was created from an earlier work by Sir Christopher Wren. It was published in Elias Ashmole's *Institution, Laws, and Ceremonies of the Order of the Garter* in 1667. The engraving shows the buildings erected in the upper ward by Edward III, claimed to be the greatest secular building campaign of the Middle Ages. Nestling at the base of the chalk cliff the eastern part of Windsor is shown, including the wooden bridge over the river Thames and several timber framed buildings fronting the river.

4 View of Windsor Castle and Town from the North – Pieter Van der Aa – 1704

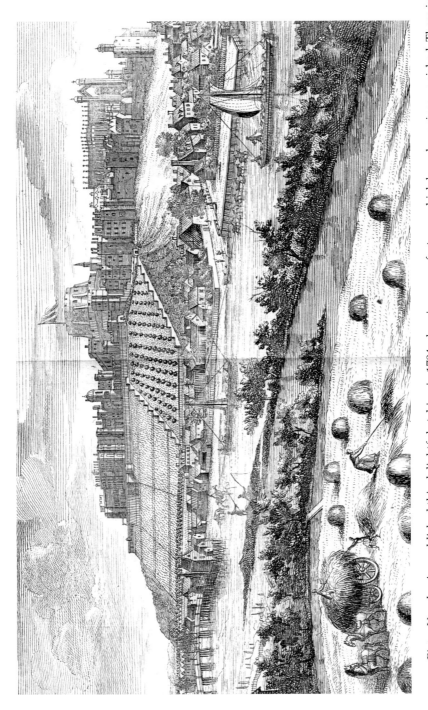

Dutch engraver Pieter Van der Aa, published this delightful etching in 1704, showing many features which have long since vanished. These include Edward III's buildings in the castle's upper ward, the interior of which was remodeled by Hugh May from 1675 to 1683 – very little now remains of May's work. The Thames in the foreground appears to be rather shallow – note the horses in the river pulling a barge. The etching shows a spacious wharf adjacent to River Street. The wooden bridge connecting Eton and Windsor is shown with an interesting built-up pier structure.

5 View of Windsor Castle and Town from the North – Leonard Knyff – 1705

The North Prospect of Winsor Castle By Mr Knife –

The riverside area of Windsor is shown slightly to the east at the bottom of the steep cliff. The timber bridge and the riverside timber revetments are also shown. This painting hangs in the castle State Apartments and was purchased by King George V in 1926. (RCIN 404917). *See Colour Plate 1.*

6 View of Windsor Castle and Town from the East – Kip & Knyff – 1709

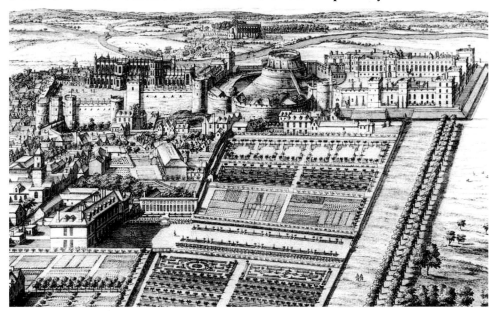

This elegant bird's eye view of Windsor Castle and parts of the town including the medieval parish church was drawn and engraved by Leonard Knyff and Johannes Kip as part of their publication called *Britannia Illustrata*. This engraving also shows Burford House. The house was given to Nell Gwyn, mistress of Charles II in 1680 and was later occupied by her son, Charles, Earl of Burford who became the 1st Duke of St Albans. The 3rd Duke of St Albans sold it to King George III in 1777; today it is the Royal Mews.

7 The Queen's Lodge – Front elevation by Sir William Chambers – 1777

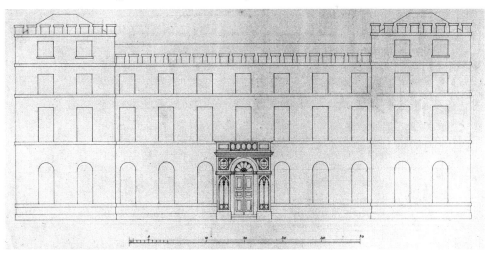

Originally known as the Queen's Garden Lodge, there was a small house which stood beneath the southern terrace of the upper ward of Windsor Castle. It was used by Queen Anne as the castle was in a bad state of repair and uninhabitable. This building was completely rebuilt by Sir William Chambers for George III, and George III himself may have had a hand in the design. The building which Sir William produced was very barrack-like in its construction. At this time the Long Walk was not connected to the castle; effectively it formed a grand entrance to the Great Park from Windsor. (RCIN 930136)

8 View of Queen's Lodge – James Fitler (after George Robertson) – 1783

The lodge was occupied by King George III and his family between 1778 and 1808, though the building work was not completed until 1782. Queen's Lodge was demolished by George IV in August 1823 to connect the Long Walk to the castle as a grand ceremonial approach. In this engraving George III and his family are shown walking along the South Terrace. Burford House can be seen in the background. (RCIN 700380)

9 Royal Palace of Windsor – Printed by Richard Sayer – 1780

This engraving shows Windsor Castle and the town of Windsor from the north. The view is dominated by an imposing seventeenth-century structure which housed Sir Samuel Moreland's water engine, constructed in 1681. The engine pumped some sixty barrels an hour up to the Terrace Walk of the castle and could supply the whole castle with water. This engine was replaced by Queen Anne in 1710 and had gone out of use by 1825.

10 The Round Tower and Upper Court of Windsor Castle c.1789

This picture illustrates a satirical piece of prose which lampoons the Clerk of Works Thomas Tildesley, and includes comments supposedly from his contemporaries. Tildesley was removed from his office by George III in 1789 due to his general rudeness and bad temper. The watercolour shows part of the restoration work at Windsor Castle carried out by George III in the late 1780s. Several key figures in the castle's restoration are shown including Thomas Tildesley (No. 1 – Clerk of Works), architect Henry Emblin (No. 5), John Slingsby (No. 6 - King's Master Mason), and Sir William Chambers (No. 11 – Surveyor General and Architect to George III). *See Colour Plate 2.*

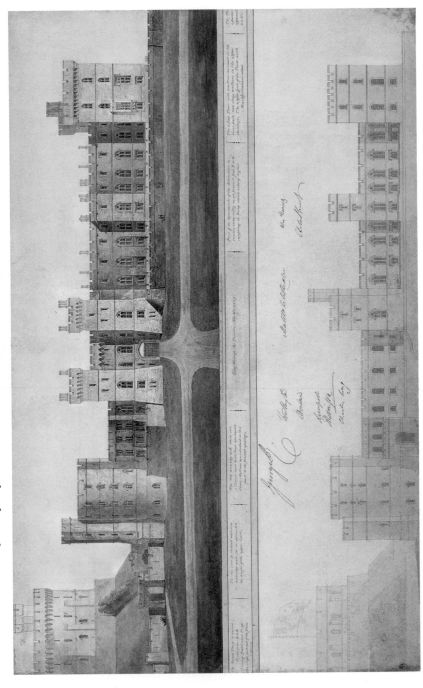

11 Jeffrey Wyatville's Elevations for the South Front of the Castle – 1824

In 1824 Jeffrey Wyatt's new plans and designs for the restoration work for Windsor Castle were selected by King George IV. He produced hand-coloured sketches of both the original state of the castle buildings together with drawings of the castle post restoration. The illustration shows Wyatville's elevation of the Round Tower and South Front before and after its restoration. (RCIN 91831) *See Colour Plate 3.*

Castle Hill & High Street

12 John Norden's Plan of Windsor showing Castle Hill and High Street – 1607

This is the earliest and most detailed street plan of Windsor. The area east of the castle is shown and includes the medieval parish church (demolished in 1820), the Market House (demolished in 1686), the town pillory and the surrounding streets and houses. The plan is inaccurate in many respects, however, as some of the town's most important buildings are missing such as the early guildhall and Sadler's market cross. *See Colour Plate 4.*

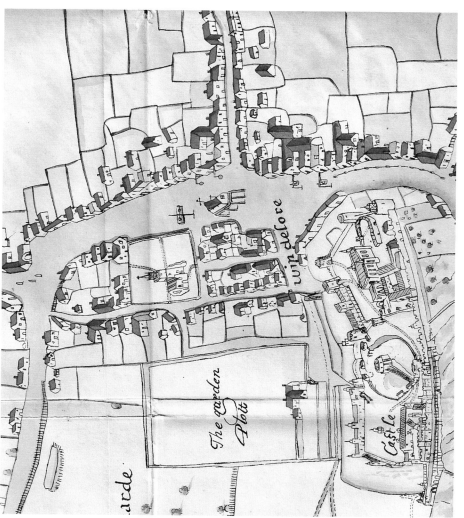

13 Ornately Decorated Arch erected at Castle Hill – March 1863

Part of a series of triumphal arches erected to celebrate the marriage of Edward Prince of Wales to Princess Alexandra of Denmark at St George's Chapel. The arch was designed and executed by a Mr Croydon. It was decorated in the Italianate style and painted to represent different shades of Sienna marble. The arch was lit by 5000 oil lamps and festooned with flags and banners. When the Royal couple arrived at the arch they were met and welcomed by the Mayor and Corporation.

14 Unveiling of Queen Victoria's Jubilee Statue – 1887

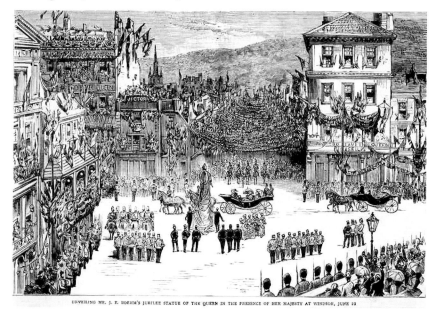

UNVEILING MR. J. E. BOEHM'S JUBILEE STATUE OF THE QUEEN IN THE PRESENCE OF HER MAJESTY AT WINDSOR, JUNE 22

The statue of Queen Victoria cast in bronze was designed and executed by Sir Edgar Boehm. It was erected in 1887 to commemorate the Queen's Golden Jubilee. The cost of £2,500 was covered by subscriptions from the people of Windsor and the surrounding districts. The Queen looks towards Peascod Street which is festooned with garlands.

15 Queen Victoria's Statue surrounded by a canopy – 1897

The canopy was erected in celebration of Queen Victoria's Diamond Jubilee in 1897 and was designed by Alfred Young Nutt who was Assistant Architect and later Surveyor of St George's Chapel. Although it looks very solid it is only made of wood and painted canvas. The Jubilee Statue was situated near to site of Sadler's Cross on the corner of Castle Hill and the High Street. The cross was erected by the town bailiff John Sadler in c.1380 and was the place where all important proclamations were announced by the Mayor and Corporation. It was also the site of Windsor's relocated market from the fifteenth century onwards. The cross was pulled down in 1691.

16 Windsor's Proclamation of Queen Elizabeth II's Accession to the Throne – 1952

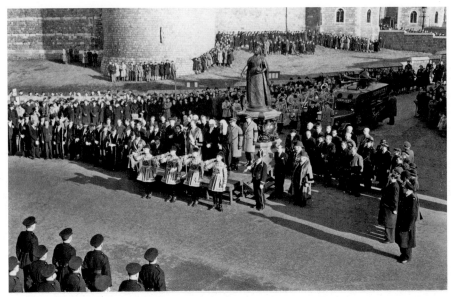

King George VI died on 6 February 1952 and at Windsor on the 8 February 1952 Princess Elizabeth was proclaimed Queen by the Mayor, Alderman R. H. Tozer in front of Queen Victoria's Jubilee Statue.

17 Market Day, High Street – Photograph by George Moore Henton – 1895

Windsor's market was held weekly on a Saturday. The photograph records the cluttered makeshift stalls which have encroached on the High Street pavement. The shops adjacent to the Guildhall are within early 17th century buildings and some of them have subterranean vaults running beneath the pavement and into the High Street.

18 Watercolour of Guildhall and High Street – William Westhall – c.1830

The painting by William Westall c.1830 shows Windsor High Street and the newly refurbished Guildhall. The Guildhall was extended in 1828-30 and the building was doubled in size. The work was carried out by James Thomas Bedborough and Robert Tebbott, who also worked with Wyatville on the refurbishment of Windsor Castle.

19 Engraving of the Interior of the Meat Market – Windsor Guildhall – 1865

During the reign of Queen Victoria it was the tradition that the Royal family at New Year would give gifts of meat and other food produce to the poor of Windsor. The poor were also given warm winter coats. In 1865 the gifts were distributed from the Guildhall but this normally took place in the Royal Riding School.

20 Royal Carriage Procession past Windsor Guildhall – 1905

King Edward VII and Queen Alexandra in Royal Procession through Windsor High Street. Note the glazed windows of the Guildhall added in 1867. A Caley & Son wagon is parked outside the Guildhall.

21 Windsor Guildhall and the Three Tuns Hotel – 1903

Windsor's first guildhall built in c.1350 (demolished. 1724) existed close to the castle and was where the Windsor Corporation met until the erection of the present guildhall in 1687. The building which now houses the Three Tuns Public House was originally known as Trinity House and was built in c. 1518. This was the meeting place of the town guild known from the 15th century as the Fraternity of the Blessed Trinity; an association of town traders focused on religious and social activities. The photograph shows soldiers who have just returned from the Boer War, preparing for a parade through Thames Street.

22 Salute the Soldier Week Inaugural Ceremony, Castle Hill – 1944

The opening ceremony of Windsor's Salute the Soldier Week was attended by the Mayor (Alfred W Bull) and Corporation of Windsor and was officially opened by Lt. General Sir Ronald Weeks, KCB (Deputy Chief of the Imperial General Staff) at Castle Hill on the 20 May 1944.

23 The Guildhall Decorated for Salute the Soldier Week – 1944

Each year during the Second World War a week was especially designated to raise money for the war effort. In 1944 Salute the Soldier Week ran from 20-27 May and raised a staggering £428,948 through contributions from the town of Windsor.

24 Artists painting in Church Street – 1900

Even today the narrow picturesque streets of St Albans Street and Church Street are painted and photographed by Windsorians and tourists alike. In this view we see Victorian artists in Church Street probably painting the view of Church Street and Windsor Castle in the background.

25 Church Street in c.1935

View of picturesque Church Street looking toward the Parish Church. To the right of the Ship was the building which held the town's first fire engine from 1803. Despite the claim, Nell Gwyn did not live in this house.

26 The Old Parish Church by John Chessell Buckler – 1814

The old medieval parish church stood on the site of the present day church. It was possibly erected c. 1130, although certainly by 1180. The church by the 16th century had major altars dedicated to the Blessed Virgin Mary and to St John the Baptist. There was also a chantry chapel dedicated to the Holy Trinity and a collection of other altars to important saints and apostles. The church also had a low central tower, which by 1479 had a clock. In the sixteenth century a wooden structure was added to the tower which contained bells and had a spire. By the beginning of the 19th century the church was said to be in a bad state of repair: it was demolished in 1820. This is a pen and ink drawing by antiquary and architect John Chessell Buckler.

27 Windsor Parish Church and its Bells during re-hanging – 1930

In 1711 a ring of eight bells was given by Samuel Masham, Cofferer to Queen Anne. The bells were cast by Richard Phelps of the Whitechapel Bell Foundry. Only three of the original bells survive today, the others were recast in 1822 after the parish church was rebuilt. This photograph was taken during the re-hanging of the bells in 1930 by Messrs. Mears and Stainbank of the Whitechapel Bell Foundry.

28 The Mayor and Corporation of Windsor processing to the Parish Church c.1920

This was an ancient custom which dates back to the mid fifteenth century when an exclusive gallery was added to the church for the Mayor and the Corporation. Borough Statutes of 1683 stipulated that seven members of the Guild should accompany the Mayor to church every Sunday. This was later reduced to once a month and today the Council process to church twice a year.

29 The Beer Dray, Church Lane – Photograph by George Moore Henton – 1894

A drayman from the Neville Reid Brewery loads beer barrels into the George IV Public House's cellar. In total contrast, adjacent to the inn is the Gordon Temperance Hotel which was run by a William Gostling. The hotel opened in the 1890s and advertised among the usual services that 'Beanfeasts and Excursionists' were catered for. The hotel was quite successful and very popular with the temperance movement. It finally closed its doors in 1925.

30 Windsor Parish Church and Flower Market – by George Moore Henton – 1895

The present day parish church was opened in 1822 and follows the foundations of its medieval predecessor. The new church was designed by architect Charles Hollis and built by Robert Tebbott and James Thomas Bedborough. The photograph also shows the adjacent florist shop owned by G Hiatt and the Ind Coope Brewery Offices.

31 Queen Victoria's Funeral Cortège passing through Windsor High Street – 1901

Queen Victoria's funeral cortège passed through Windsor High Street on 4 February 1901, after the lying in state in the Albert Memorial Chapel. In this photograph the cortège is seen passing the Union Hotel and the London County Bank in the High Street en-route to her burial place at the mausoleum at Frogmore. Note the wooden cobbles on the street.

32 The Theatre Royal, High Street – 1805

A so-called 'Theatre Royal' was found in a converted barn in a farmyard at the bottom of Peascod Street in around 1778, but Windsor's first purpose-built theatre was erected by a Mr Bowen and opened in Windsor High Street in 1793. It was very small, but popular with George III. The High Street building which housed the theatre was later used as a place of worship by the Windsor Congregationalist Church, while a new theatre opened on its present site in 1814. In 1832 The Congregationalists moved to a new church in William Street and the High Street building was demolished.

33 'Lord' George Sanger's Circus Parade along High Street c.1890

Circus parades were very popular in the English provincial town and Windsor was no exception. They were a great favourite with the Royal family. Sanger's circus was asked to perform in Windsor Castle and when the circus had finished Queen Victoria requested that the show be repeated.

34 Post Office and High Street c.1905

A Post Office stood in this area from 1841. This new building was designed by Scottish architect John Lessels who was Surveyor of the Royal Palaces. It was built by J Dorey of Brentford and opened by the Postmaster General the Rt. Hon. Henry Raikes MP on 19 February 1887. Note the wooden hackney carriage shelter in the distance. The Post Office was moved to new premises in Peascod Street in 1966.

35 Windsor Post Office viewed from Park Street c.1972

The Post Office building viewed from Park Street during its final days before demolition in 1972.

36 Site of the Old Windsor Post office after demolition c.1972

The blank space where the Post Office once stood gives a rare glimpse of the eastern elevation of the parish church.

37 High Street c.1915 with a car parked in the middle of the street.

Caleys had taken over part of the premises of Dyson and Denyer. This building was only used for a short time after which it became the Midland Bank in 1919, and is now the HSBC Bank.

38 Caleys shortly before closure in July 2006

Sometime before 1813 Maria Caley ran a millinery and dressmaking shop in Thames Street, Windsor. She then moved to Castle Hill where her sister Charlotte Noke was in the same business, and brother John Caley was a silk mercer. When John married in 1820 his wife Mary Ann joined the business. Maria and Charlotte left to help their husbands who both ran allied businesses and in 1823 John and Mary Ann moved to the premises in the High Street opposite the Guildhall which was known as Caleys for 183 years. The shop was run by the sons and grandsons of John and Mary Ann Caley and the wives always played significant roles until 1919 when it was sold to the American H. Gordon Selfridge. In 1940 the Selfridge family sold all their provincial stores including Caleys to the John Lewis Partnership. In 1951-2 the frontage was rebuilt in the Georgian style. The premises were continually expanding and by the time the shop closed it occupied five High Street buildings. Caley's finally ceased trading on Saturday 15 July 2006 and is sadly missed by all Windsorians.

39 Funeral procession of King Edward VII – 1910

Over the last century Windsor had many events which spectators flocked to see and viewing space was at a premium. To cater for their needs many shops, businesses and hotels in Windsor allowed people to stand on what appear to be extremely rickety balconies on their upper floors. This photograph shows viewing platforms at Caleys and at the Harte and Garter Hotel (which looks as if it is in a state of collapse!).

40 Entrance to Windsor and Eton GWR Railway Station – 1908

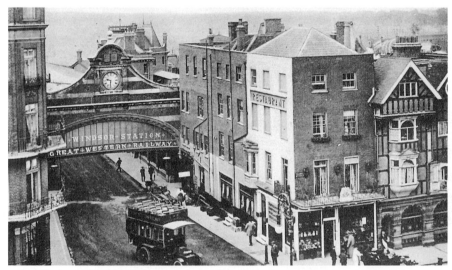

The Windsor & Eton Central Railway Station, opened on 8 October 1849, marked the completion of the branch line from Slough to Windsor. To make way for the railway, the notorious George Street with its many pubs, bawdy houses and resident prostitutes, was demolished and became Station Approach. The new branch line meant the Queen and her entourage could now travel direct from Paddington. In 1897, for the Queen's Jubilee, this splendid arch was erected and the station was refurbished. On the corner of Station Approach and Thames Street is the fashionable Layton's Restaurant. It played host to a luncheon for dignitaries before the Marathon of the 1908 Olympic Games.

41 Queen Victoria's Waiting Room – Great Western Railway Station c.1899

Royal waiting rooms at railway stations were sumptuous affairs as can be seen by this late Victorian photograph. This is the Royal Waiting room constructed for the Windsor and Eton Central Railway Station in 1897; it was later extended in 1902 and used by royalty until 1936.

42 The Funeral of Queen Victoria – Windsor and Eton GWR Railway Station – 1901

Queen Victoria died on 22nd January 1901 at Osborne House on the Isle of Wight. Her body was brought to Windsor via Portsmouth and London. The final leg of her journey to Windsor was by rail from Paddington and took place on 2 February 1901.

As the crowned heads of Europe formed up behind the coffin the horses that were trying to pull it could not get a foothold and slipped on the wet, icy, wooden cobbles. The Royal Marines came forward and pulled the hearse up the hill to the castle with ropes. They still do that for the funeral of the Monarch (see no. 31). The wooden cobbles were taken up in the 1940s.

Park Street

43 Park Street looking towards the High Street c.1900

Park Street was originally a thoroughfare to London via Frogmore, Old Windsor and Staines. Over the centuries it has been known by several names. Its earliest name, probably from the twelfth century, was *More Strate* or Moor Street because it led to *Frog Moor*. In 1604 it was known by the imposing name of *Cuthorse Well Street*, where a public well had been erected. The origin of the name Cuthorse is unknown. By 1640 it had changed again to Pound Street, the site of the Parish Pound where stray animals were kept and released to their owners for a fee. It was also used to keep animals before slaughter in the butchers' shambles on the town market. The name Park Street does not appear until 1742. Many of the facades which can be seen in this photograph date from the Georgian period.

44 Park Street c.1890

Park Street looking towards the New Inn. (See no. 47)

45 Lower Park Street c.1940?

The buildings on Park Street are all of particular architectural merit and show influence of the great Georgian architects such as John Nash and Sir Robert Taylor and they emulated the fashionable residences to be found in London. This picture shows Park Street looking towards the Long Walk.

46 The New Inn Hotel shortly before demolition c.1930

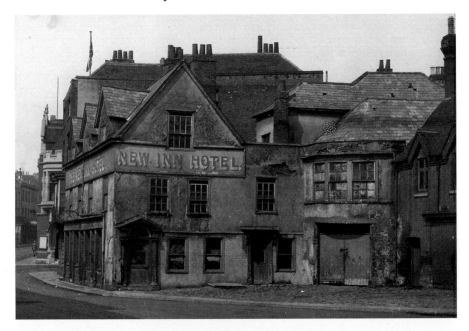

In the late 1920s the New Inn Hotel had become derelict and unsafe. It was demolished in the autumn of 1931. During the demolition of the hotel a blocked up room was found containing the skeleton of a large, 300 year old dog, and a musket. A number of coins dating to the reign of Queen Elizabeth I were also found.

47 The New Inn Hotel c.1900

The New Inn, or the King's Arms as it was originally known, was a coaching inn or posting house which dated to the fifteenth century and served the old road from Windsor to London. In 1802 after a day of stag hunting King George III was taken to the tap room for refreshment before returning to the King's Stables at the rear of the inn. During the nineteenth century travellers could hire coaches or open carriages from the inn. By 1900 it was known as the New Inn Hotel. *See Colour Plate 5.*

Sheet Street

48 Sheet Street looking north showing the site of the Infantry Barracks, Watercolour by Paul Sandby – 1777

Sheet Street dates from the early twelfth century, the name 'Sheet' coming from Old English and relating to one of the town's open common fields which lay to the east of this street. Sandby's watercolour shows Sheet Street as an idyllic country lane with a few small cottages along it. Sheet Street became more of a residential area once the military barracks were built in 1795. (RCIN 914608). *See Colour Plate 6.*

49 Sheet Street looking North – c.1935

This photograph shows roughly the same view as the Sandby watercolour on the previous page. On the left hand side of the road is the earliest phase of building of the Victoria Barracks dating from 1795 (bus outside). In the foreground is the site of the Pesthouse which became a workhouse in 1739, the borough gaol in 1843 and the police station from 1856 to 1902. After that it became part of the barracks. On the opposite side of the road is the now-demolished Five Bells Public House on the corner of Sheet Street and Brook Street. Note how narrow Sheet Street was at that time. It was not until 1938 that Sheet Street was widened.

50 Victoria Barracks c.1970

The original infantry barracks, built between 1798 and 1799, were demolished in 1985.

51 Guards Marching past Victoria Barracks along Sheet Street – Photograph by George Moore Henton – 1894

A maid and children watch as soldiers march along Sheet Street past Victoria Barracks.

52 The Parade Ground – Victoria Barracks – 1902

Scots Guards on parade under Lieutenant General Paul Methuen in the Victoria Barracks after returning from the Boer War. In the background are the barrack blocks erected in 1865-67.

53 Coldstream Guards at Play – Victoria Barracks – 1906

Coldstream Guards at play, Windsor Barracks

This 1906 postcard shows guardsmen playing cricket on the parade ground. In the background are Victorian barrack blocks built between 1865 and 1867. *See Colour Plate 7.*

54 Victoria Barracks – 1970

The Victoria Barracks were extended once again in 1916. This extension was built over two streets Love Lane and Wellington Square. The barrack block in this photograph is viewed from Dagmar Road. The extension is in the background. The Victoria Barracks were totally demolished in 1985 and rebuilt. *See Colour Plate 8.*

55 Royal Albert Institute – 1870

The Royal Albert Institute started life as the Literary, Scientific and Mechanics Institute and opened in Sheet Street in 1835. In 1870 a new building was erected adjacent to the Mechanics Institute on the site of the Royal Mews in Sheet Street. The architects were Messrs. H F Bacon and E Ingress Bell of London and it was built by Mr Woodbridge of Maidenhead. The building was created in the Tudor style with a niche above the entrance which held a marble statue of Prince Albert. It contained reading and class rooms and a large hall for concerts and grand balls capable of holding 500 people. It also housed a local history museum.

56 Royal Albert Institute shortly before demolition – c.1976

The Royal Albert Institute was demolished in 1977. All that remains from the original building is a replica of the statue of Prince Albert which stands in a niche above the entrance to the present building. The original statue by the Italian sculptor Romanelli is now in the entrance porch of Holy Trinity Church in Trinity Place. *See Colour Plate 9.*

Thames Street

57 Thames Street – 1906

A view of Thames Street from its junction with High Street. The northern side of the street is dominated by the Curfew Tower and the curtain wall of the castle. Note the small domed structure used as an information booth and notice board until the 1960s. Further down the hill across from the Station Approach are horse-drawn cabs waiting to take railway passengers on to their final destinations. *See Colour Plate 10.*

58 Thames Street– 1950

A general view of Thames Street in 1950. The dome on the information booth has now been removed and has been crenellated.

59 Thames Street – General View – 1905

The shops on Thames Street catered for every need of the Edwardian household. They sold everything from musical instruments to tobacco. This view shows several such businesses including the White Hart Hotel (now the Harte and Garter), Dyson's the jewellers and Parsons the tobacconists. *See Colour Plate 11.*

60 Dyson's Jewellers and Piano shop – Thames Street – 1902

In this view Dyson's and Sons, jewellers, and the adjacent piano shop are shown in the background as soldiers returning from the Boer War march along Thames Street.

61 Dyson's Clock in the Pavement, Thames Street – c.1955

This became one of Windsor's landmarks and was put in the pavement by shop owner Cyril Dyson in 1950. The clock was one of only two pavement clocks known to have existed in the world. It remained on view outside Dyson's shop for over thirty years. A new clock is planned to be installed in 2010 by The Royal Borough of Windsor and Maidenhead.

62 Boots Cash Chemists – Thames Street – 1904

Boots Cash Chemists was another landmark of Edwardian Windsor. It was famous for its large illuminated green shop sign which covered most of the upper storeys of the building. It proclaimed Boots to be the largest retail chemists in the world.

The North Prospect
of Windsor Castle By
Mr Knyfe

Plate 1 – View of Windsor Castle and Town from the North – Leonard Knyff – 1705

Plate 2. The Round Tower and Upper Court of Windsor Castle c.1789

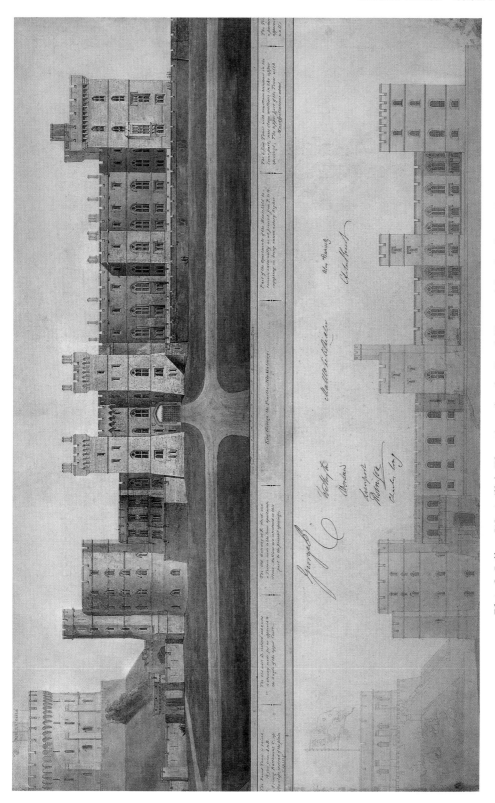

Plate 3. Jeffrey Wyatville's Elevations for the South Front of the Castle – 1824

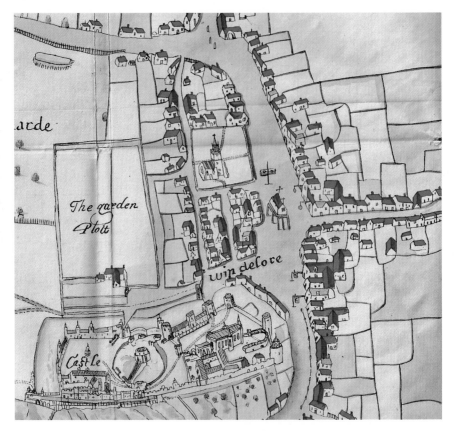

Plate 4. John Norden's Plan of Windsor showing Castle Hill and High Street – 1607

Plate 5. The New Inn Hotel c.1900

Plate 6. Sheet Street looking north showing the site of the Infantry Barracks
Watercolour by Paul Sandby – 1777

Plate 7. Coldstream Guards at Play – Victoria Barracks – 1906

Plate 8. Victoria Barracks – 1970

Plate 9. Royal Albert Institute shortly before demolition – c.1976

Plate 10. Thames Street – 1906

Plate 11. Thames Street – General View – 1905

Plate 12. River Street towards Thames Street.
Watercolour by George Moore Henton 1908

Plate 13. North side of Thames Street – Houses built in the moat of Windsor Castle. Watercolour by Paul Sandby, c1780

Plate 14. Lower Thames Street – Houses built in the Castle Ditch, Watercolour by John Preston Neale – 1846

Plate 15. Mr Isherwood's Brewery – Watercolour by Paul Sandby – 1770

Plate 16. The Timber Windsor Bridge c.1818

Plate 17. Windsor Bridge c.1830

Plate 18. Windsor Bridge with traffic – 1936

Plate 19. Alexandra Gardens – 1902

53721.

Riverside Gardens, Windsor.

Plate 20. Riverside Gardens – 1908

Plate 21. Peascod Street, Watercolour by Louise Rayner c.1897

Plate 22. Peascod Street – Watercolour by George Moore Henton – 1907

Plate 23. Fire and Police Station St Leonard's Road – 1907

Plate 24. The Kipling Memorial Building, Alma Road c.1970

63 E V Tull's Restaurant, Thames Street – 1930

Tull's Restaurant was particularly known for its confectionery and cakes and received a Royal Warrant both from Queen Victoria and also King George V. The restaurant boasted fine views of the River Thames and attracted tourists and locals alike. Some of the cakes which Tull's were famous for can be seen artistically displayed in the ground floor shop window. Tull's also had a bakery in Peascod Street.

64 Lower Thames Street – John Lessels – c.1863

Drawing by John Lessels of Thames Street at its junction with
Bier Lane. Lessels was Surveyor of the Royal Palaces and also
designed the Post Office in the High Street. This view has a distinct
rural feel to it with sheep and cattle meandering down Thames
Street (RCIN 917409)

65 River Street towards Thames Street. Watercolour by George Moore Henton 1908

River Street was originally called New Street and dates from the early thirteenth century. It later became known as Beer Street possibly named after a brewery located on the street. There may have also been a connection with Andrew Beerman who endowed a Windsor almshouse in 1523. By 1791 it was known as Bier Lane, a corruption of 'beer', as the street had no association with funerals. It was renamed River Street in 1883. *See Colour Plate 12.*

66 Organ Grinder and Cutler, River Street. Photograph by George Moore Henton – 1894

View of River Street looking south towards the river. The organ grinder and the cutler have left their machines in the street while the horse is feeding. Note the sign, above the men's heads, recording the height of the very recent 1894 floods as an incredible nine feet deep. The flood was the greatest of the nineteenth century.

67 Cottages known as Red Lion Row, off Bier Lane c.1880

There were several rows of small cottages which ran off Bier Lane. These included Distill House Row, Garden Court and Red Lion Row. In the late 18th century Bier Lane was known for a short while as Red Lion Street (named after the Red Lion Inn on the corner of its junction with the High Street). By 1926 the majority of the buildings were unfit for habitation and were cleared away. The land was flattened and made into Windsor's first car park. (See no. 68)

68 The River Street Car Park c.1935

Aerial View of the River Street Car Park taken from the Library Terrace of Windsor Castle c.1935.

69 16th century timber framed buildings, River Street c.1980

These buildings once fronted onto a wharf at the end of River Street. In 1985 they were demolished and the area made into a car park.

70 View of a timber wharf which was located at the end of River Street – 1704

This view is taken from the very detailed picture of Windsor Castle and town by Van der Aa. The wharf was where goods which were transported along the Thames could be unloaded and bought up into the town. This wharf was later replaced by Jenning's Wharf in the nineteenth century.

71 North side of Thames Street – Houses built in the moat of Windsor Castle, Watercolour by Paul Sandby – c1780

Buildings started to be built in the castle ditch in Thames Street from the fourteenth century onwards. From the sixteenth century these were progressively extended up to the Henry VIII Gateway. The remains of the ditch functioned as an open sewer to the rear of these properties. This watercolour shows the houses built on the area at the junction of Castle Hill and High Street. Note the Georgian façade which has been built onto an earlier seventeenth-century building. This was part of a general improvement scheme where the shops and buildings were updated to the latest taste in fashion during the 1780s and 90s. The main reason for this was that George III and his family had taken up residence at Windsor after earlier Hanoverians had neglected the town. (RCIN 914547) *See Colour Plate 13.*

72 Lower Thames Street – Houses built in the Castle Ditch, Watercolour by John Preston Neale – 1846

View of the houses, shops and public houses built within the Castle ditch at Lower Thames Street. Note the earlier roof of the Curfew Tower. The roof was replaced during the restoration of the west front of the castle by Anthony Salvin in 1863. *See Colour Plate 14.*

73 Lower Thames Street (Artist Unknown) c1800

Houses built against the castle wall in lower Thames Street.

74 Lower Thames Street c.1910

By the middle of the nineteenth century many of the buildings against the castle wall were in a bad state of repair and those adjacent to the Henry VIII gateway were removed as part of the renovation of the castle by Wyatville. Between 1851 and 1857 the houses built in the ditch further down Thames Street were pulled down as part of a general improvement scheme for the town of Windsor. The area where these houses once stood was either paved or grassed over, creating the present day landscape. In this view the canopy of the Theatre Royal can be seen.

75 The Theatre Royal, Thames Street on fire – 1908

On Monday 17 February 1908 the Theatre Royal caught fire and it took both the Windsor and the Eton fire brigades to quench the flames. The fire damage was mainly confined to the backstage area. An asbestos fire curtain stopped the flames from reaching the auditorium; however, the auditorium was badly affected by water damage.

76 Fire Damage done to the Theatre Royal – 1908

A fireman inspects the charred remains of stage area from the dress circle of the theatre.

77 Fire Damage done to the Theatre Royal – 1908

View of the fire damage to the stage and roof of the theatre. The theatre was owned by Sir William Shipley and Major Reginald Shipley who had just spent the last few years renovating the theatre. After the fire the charred remains of the 1815 building were demolished and a new larger theatre designed by Frank Verity ARIBA arose from the ashes. The theatre reopened in December 1910.

78 The Royalty Cinema, Lower Thames Street c.1930

In April 1932 the Theatre Royal closed down and a month later opened as the 'Royalty Cinema'. Between September 1933 and May 1934 it returned to being a theatre, but closed again after eight months due to a lack of funds. The Royalty finally closed down in 1938 and reopened as the Theatre Royal with a permanent repertory company.

79a Auditorium of the Royalty Cinema c.1930

79b The Foyer of the Royalty Cinema c.1930

80 Mr Isherwood's Brewery – Watercolour by Paul Sandby – 1770

From as early as the fifteenth century brewing was Windsor's principal industry. Henry Isherwood's Brewery in Lower Thames Street was Windsor's first brewery and was founded c.1720. In 1780 Henry Isherwood sold the brewery to the Ramsbottom family. (RCIN 914596) *See Colour Plate 15.*

81 John Ramsbottom's Brewery and Lower Thames Street – J C Nattes – c.1798

Old Bank House was built in c.1758 for Henry Isherwood. It is thought that building was erected by Sir Robert Taylor. It was used partly as brewery offices and partly as accommodation for the brewery owner. The Ramsbottom family acquired the house in 1780. John Ramsbottom later established a Bank on the premises. This was known as the Windsor Bank. The medieval house with the jettied frontage next to Old Bank House was occupied by a lay clerk whose job it was to unlock the Gate of a Hundred Steps. The building was the last one within the castle ditch to be cleared in 1857. (RCIN 917389)

82 John Ramsbottom's Brewery c.1815

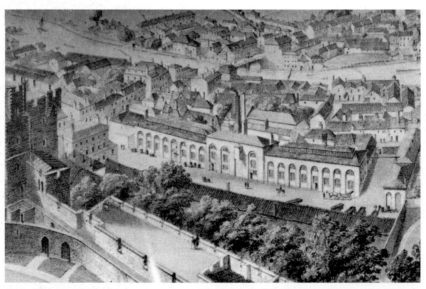

View of the brewery from Windsor Castle showing the greatly expanded premises. In 1837 the brewery and bank were taken over by Neville Reid and Co. The London Brewery Noakes and Company purchased the Thames Street brewery in 1918 and sold it again in 1930 to Courage & Company. It finally closed its gates in 1962 marking the end of over two hundred years of continuous brewing on the site.

83 Demolition of Part of Courage's Brewery, Lower Thames Street c.1933

Around 1933 a portion of Courage's Brewery was demolished to make way for the George V Memorial.

84 The Unveiling of the George V Memorial – 1937

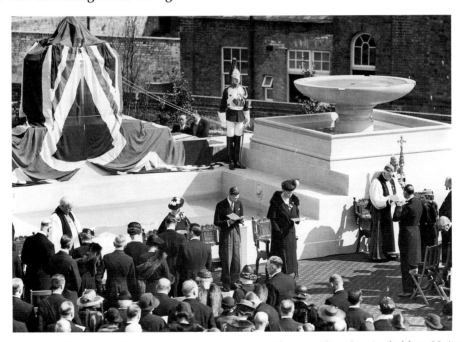

King George VI, Queen Elizabeth and Queen Mary at the unveiling Service held on 23 April 1937. It was constructed from designs by the architect Sir Edwin Lutyens and financed by public subscription. Notice the absence of trees overshadowing the memorial as they do today. It became very dirty and derelict but has recently been refurbished.

85 Exterior of the Playhouse Cinema, Lower Thames Street – c.1932

The Windsor Playhouse Cinema was designed by the celebrated cinema architect Robert Cromie. It took six months to complete and opened on Boxing Day 1928.

86 Playhouse Cinema Auditorium c.1932

The cinema which Robert Cromie designed was highly advanced in both its architecture and in technology. This imposing auditorium could seat 1,500 people. It had a special acoustic chamber behind the stage to give its audience better sound clarity. The original colour scheme for the cinema was silver, jade green and apricot.

87 Playhouse Cinema Stage and Organ c.1932

88 Lower Thames Street from Windsor Bridge showing the ABC Cinema – c.1974

When the Playhouse Cinema was originally constructed great care was taken to give it a Georgian style frontage so it would blend in with surviving eighteenth century architecture of Lower Thames Street.

Windsor Bridge and Riverside

89 Windsor Bridge, Town and Castle. Extract from Van der Aa engraving, 1704

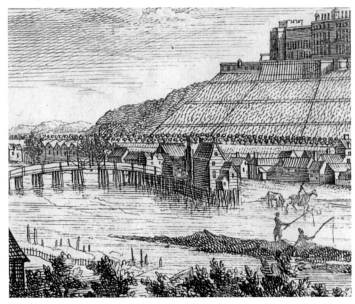

Windsor bridge is first mentioned in 1192, although it may have existed at a slightly earlier date, and was constructed of timber. The Thames was a major highway for trade coming in and out of the port of London. At various times throughout the middle ages the King gave the town the right to collect tolls from boats passing under the bridge and travellers going over it, to affect repairs. The bridge was one of the town's most important economic assets.

90 The Timber Windsor Bridge c.1818

By the beginning of the nineteenth century the timber Windsor Bridge had become dilapidated and it was decided to take it down and construct a sturdier and wider one. This watercolour shows the timber bridge a few years before it was demolished in February 1822. *See Colour Plate 16.*

91 Windsor Bridge c.1830

The new bridge was designed by Charles Hollis and constructed using cast iron. On 22 June 1822 the cornerstone of the new bridge was laid with Masonic ceremony by Frederick Duke of York. The bridge had cost £15.000 to build and opened to traffic on 1 June 1824. *See Colour Plate 17.*

92 Windsor Bridge and Jubilee Arch – Photograph by George Moore Henton – 1897

This view shows a crowd of people crossing the bridge between Windsor and Eton. In the background is the Jubilee Arch erected to celebrate Queen Victoria's Diamond Jubilee. (See no. 94)

93 Jubilee Arch, Lower, Thames Street – 1887

This arch was erected to celebrate Queen Victoria's Golden Jubilee in 1887. The Old Toll House and bridge can be seen in the background. (RCIN 2915941)

94 Jubilee Arch, Lower Thames Street – 1897

Jubilee Arch designed and erected by A Y Nutt in 1897 in celebration of Queen Victoria's Diamond Jubilee. The arch was situated at the Lower Thames Street end of Windsor Bridge adjacent to the old toll house. Through the arch are the decorated shops and buildings in celebration of the Jubilee. The statue represents the young Queen Victoria.

95 The Old Toll House, Lower Thames Street c.1830

Since medieval times tolls had been collected both for going over and under Windsor Bridge. Towards the end of the 19th century Windsor's inhabitants protested against the levying of tolls. The toll gates were removed from the bridge in December 1898 after much campaigning under the leadership of Joseph Taylor. This view shows the old toll house converted into a tobacconist and souvenir shop and in the background is the Riverholme Hotel.

96 Windsor Bridge with traffic – 1936

Traffic crossing Windsor Bridge was once a familiar sight as shown in this 1936 view. By the 1930s cracks started to appear in the main infrastructure of the bridge and a weight limit was imposed as an attempt to stop further deterioration. During the war years this appears to have been ignored as heavy military vehicles often crossed it. Traffic was finally banned on 10 April 1970 and the bridge was pedestrianised. *See Colour Plate 18.*

97 The Bridge's Service Garage, Thameside – 1947

The floods of 1947 were so great that, when they eventually subsided, the banks of the Thames collapsed in places, as shown in this photograph. This normally very busy promenade along the Thames was cordoned off. In the background is The Bridge's Service Garage and the tall double-gabled building which once housed the offices of Denny's the bakers.

98 Windsor Bridge covered in tarpaulin during the great freeze of 1963

In 1963 the River Thames froze over. To prevent frost damage to the pipes carrying water from Tangier Island, Eton, the whole bridge was draped in tarpaulin. To the left of the bridge is the rear of the old Toll House.

99 The Ladies Swimming Baths – 1904

The Ladies Swimming Baths were constructed in 1904. The baths were fed by the water of the Thames. In 1909 they were taken over by Windsor Corporation and renamed the Western Baths. A successful ladies swimming team was formed in 1912. The baths closed down in the 1930s but were later reused for a short while.

100 Alexandra Gardens — 1902

The land for the gardens was purchased in 1895 with the view of establishing a permanent open space for the people of Windsor. On 15 July 1902 Alexandra Gardens were opened by Princess Christian, Queen Victoria's daughter and Queen Alexandra's sister-in-law. A tree was planted in the park to commemorate the Coronation of Edward VII and Queen Alexandra, shortly after its opening. *See Colour Plate 19.*

101 Riverside Gardens – 1908

Riverside Gardens, Windsor.

53721.

The Thameside paths have always been popular with Windsorians and tourists. The Riverside Gardens started life as a tow path, but from the end of the nineteenth century was adapted into a smart riverside promenade with two paths separated by a bank and seats at regular intervals. There was also an opportunity to hire rowing boats. This 1908 view shows how busy Windsor's riverside was. Note the crowded Windsor Bridge in the distance. *See Colour Plate 20.*

Peascod Street, William Street, Victoria Street & St Leonard's Road

102 Peascod Street, Watercolour by Louise Rayner c.1897

Louise Rayner painted several vibrant watercolour views of Windsor towards the end of the century. This view shows the upper part of Peascod Street looking towards the Castle. *See Colour Plate 21.*

103 Corner of Peascod Street and High Street c.1932

Peascod Street was probably laid out shortly after Windsor Castle had been constructed. The earliest mention of the Street is *Pescrofte Strat* in c.1100. The name is derived from an area where peas were cultivated. Many of Windsor's early streets were very narrow, and over the years they were widened, which meant in some cases buildings were pulled down to accommodate the widening schemes. This was the case at the top of Peascod Street where in 1933 the two buildings on the corner of High Street and Peascod Street were demolished. They were John Manley's picture frame shop which had a handsome Victorian shop front. The shop had been run by the Manley family since 1910 and opened when the drapers Denyer and Dyson closed down. The other building to be demolished was the corner building which had a fine Elizabethan jettied frontage. This had been occupied by A C Caffryn, a Gentleman's tailor and outfitter. These two shops were replaced by a single building which had an extra floor.

104 Peascod Street c.1905

General view of Peascod Street looking towards Clewer. In this view is the Star and Garter Commercial Hotel on the right.

105 Peascod Street – 1917

View of Peascod Street looking towards the castle. Windsor Electricity Works can be seen on the right and the Star and Garter Commercial Hotel on the left with Elliot's Leather Stores further up the hill. Note the milk churn and cart by the side of the pavement.

106 The Star and Garter Inn, Peascod Street c.1960

The Star and Garter Inn dates back to at least 1550 when it was known as the *Hartshorn*. In 1630 its name changed to *The Black Bear*. During the eighteenth century it became a coaching inn and had a yard with stabling and guest accommodation. Open carriages could be hired from the inn. During the twentieth century it was known as the Star and Garter Commercial Hotel and was a well-known entertainment venue. By 1925 the hotel was famous as an international training ground for young boxers and in 1951 the legendary boxer Sugar Ray Robinson spent five days training there before a major fight in London. From 1960 to 1964 the hotel hosted the Ricky Tick Club. Many famous bands performed there including The Who, Jimi Hendrix and Pink Floyd. The Star and Garter Hotel was demolished to make way for a MacFisheries shop and chemist in 1974.

107 Peascod Street c.1910

Another view of the upper portion of Peascod Street. On the right Elliot's Leather Stores and the 'Castle Toilet Saloon' can be seen, while on the left is Williamson's the Tobacconists. Note the array of different forms of lighting outside the shops.

108 The Bull Inn, Peascod Street – 1904

The Bull Inn (later known as the Bull Hotel) was another early inn dating from at least the seventeenth century. In 1904 the inn was run by Mr C J Lovejoy. Advertisements on the exterior show that the hotel offered loose boxes, livery and stabling. Lock up coach houses were available for rent and were the equivalent of the lock up garages of today. The façade of the Bull Hotel still remains but the interior has been totally refurbished to accommodate a new shop.

109 W J Daniel & Co, Peascod Street. – 1930

Walter James Daniel opened his first shop in Uxbridge in 1901. In 1918 his son Charles purchased a small shop in Peascod Street for his sister Mabel. The Daniel family extended the store by purchasing adjacent premises in 1924. In about 1929 a further shop was bought to enlarge the Peascod Street frontage. This view shows the rather jumbled street scene which made up the Daniel shop and the display for their winter sale.

110 W J Daniel & Co, Peascod Street. – c.1955

This view of c.1955 shows a newly erected modern frontage to the Daniel shop. The three shops which originally made up the Peascod Street frontage have been unified into one. In the 1950s the Daniel family purchased a row of six cottages at the rear of the property. These were demolished and the back of the shop was used as a car park. An extension on the site of the car park was added to the store in 1979 giving them an entrance from the newly-built King Edward Court shopping precinct.

111 Windsor Fire Brigade and Fire Engine, Peascod Street – c.1925

The Windsor Fire Brigade was founded in 1867 from a band of volunteers. This remained a voluntary Brigade until 1939 when it was merged into National Fire Service. In this photograph the Windsor Fire Brigade and their latest fire engine the *Princess Mary* (being used as a hearse) parade in a funeral procession. In the background are the Empire Cinema and Curry's Cycle Company.

112 Peascod Street with the Windsor Cinema in the foreground – c.1930

The Regal Cinema was originally known simply as the 'Windsor Cinema' when it opened its doors in February 1913. This was Windsor's first purpose-built cinema and was built on the site of a grocer's shop. The cinema was built in 10 weeks and could hold 600 people. The whole building including the frontage was illuminated by electric light. In 1931 the Windsor Cinema was renamed the Regal and was refurbished. The Regal remained open until January 1969 when it became a bingo hall, a fate which befell many of the country's early picture palaces. The cinema was demolished ten years later in 1979 to make way for a new Boots the Chemists.

113 Peascod Street – Photographed by George Moore Henton – 1896

An animated photographic view of Lower Peascod Street which captures a lost era of horse-drawn traffic which was the norm at turn of the century.

114 The Alexandra Coffee Tavern – 1897

The Alexandra Coffee Tavern opened in Peascod Street in 1897 and was run by William McDonald until his death in 1900 when it was taken over by his wife until 1915. It then became a hatter's shop run by J G Hills.

115 Peascod Street – Watercolour by George Moore Henton – 1907

Lower Peascod Street by George Moore Henton was based on his own photograph (See No. 113). The watercolour shows a view of the Sun Inn, the Alexandra Coffee Tavern and the Crown Hotel on the right hand of the street and opposite, Hill & Son, Gun makers. At the top of the street is Queen Victoria's Golden Jubilee statue. *See Colour Plate 22.*

116 Wellman Brothers and Co., Peascod Street c.1930

Wellman's stood on the corner of William Street and Peascod Street and was founded by ironmonger Anthony Wellman in 1825. The shop was later taken over by his three sons, John, Edward and Alfred. The brothers were able to offer services in bell hanging, general ironmongery and white and black smithing. The company held a warrant as heating engineers to the royal family. The building was designed by the Windsor firm of architects Edgington & Spink in 1929. Wellman's shop closed during the mid 1970s.

117 John Canning's Brewery, Peascod Street – 1846

A rare view of the Peascod Street elevation of the Royal Brewery and Tap in 1846. This brewery was started in the 1780s by the Twinch family. In 1846 it was being run by brothers Frederick and John Twinch. In 1870 they sold the brewery to John Canning who renamed it the Royal Brewery after he received a warrant as brewer and maltster to Queen Victoria. In 1921 it was acquired by London brewer Noakes & Co. who transferred their London operation to Windsor. The brewery closed down in 1930 when all of the Noakes assets were purchased by Courage & Co. Ltd.

118 J Isaacs Furniture Shop, Peascod Street c.1955

After the Noakes's brewery had closed down in 1930 the building was sold to William Creak who opened a second-hand furniture shop. In the early 1950s Creak's was bought by J Isaacs to add a Windsor branch to their expanding empire of furniture shops which had begun in Slough in 1865.

119 J Isaacs Furniture Shop, Peascod Street c.1965

In the early 1960s the Isaacs Furniture shop was given a modern unified shop front with a heightened roof line which totally swept away the old brewery façade. The frontage of the adjacent old Brewery tap building was retained. Though concealed, the original hatch into the old 'tun room' still survives. In 1980-81 the furniture store moved into William Street and the old shop which fronted onto Peascod Street was divided into two shops with offices above. The Isaacs Furniture shop in William Street ceased trading in 1987 and the company became purely a property investment business.

120 Lower Peascod Street c.1910

View of the shops and buildings of lower Peascod Street in c.1910. Peascod Street was resurfaced shortly before this view was photographed. The cobbles apparent in earlier views have been removed. In 1928 Peascod Street was widened to accommodate the increased motor traffic.

121 Darvilles, Peascod Street – 1896

Darvilles tea and grocery shop opened in 1860. It quickly established itself as the main grocery store in Windsor and by the 1960s had many branches throughout the town. Darvilles have held their Royal Warrant since 1946. Note the staff in their long white aprons outside the shop.

122 Darville & Son Ltd, Peascod Street c.1927

Darvilles also carried a large range of china, glass and earthenware goods as well as groceries and tea. This view shows Darvilles new shop front c.1927.

123 William Street – 1974

William Street was named after King William IV who came to the throne in 1830. Between 1975 and 1978 almost the whole of William Street was demolished to make way for new shops, offices, and a nightclub. This involved the removal of a complete row of houses, a church, a hotel, several shops and a garage. Many of the houses which were demolished dated from the 1830s. This photograph shows a row of early cottages shortly before demolition in 1975.

124 Falcon Hotel and Coffee Shop, William Street– 1974

The Falcon Commercial Hotel opened in 1915 in what was a warehouse and store previously owned by Wellman Brothers. The hotel stood on the same site for sixty years and was demolished in 1975. This view shows the Falcon Hotel and adjoining houses shortly before their demolition.

125 United Reformed Church, William Street – 1974

The Congregational Church opened in William Street on the 1 May 1833 after moving from the cramped Theatre Royal site in the High Street. This building was demolished in 1975 along with most of the surrounding buildings. The Congregational Church had become the United Reformed Church in 1972 and a new building opened in 1979 on the same site.

126 United Reformed Church, William Street – 1975

The United Reform Church during demolition in 1975.

127 Barker's Garage, William Street – 1974

Barker's Garage was a familiar site on the corner of William Street and Victoria Street until 1974. The Contact Garage had opened on the site in 1922. From 1928 three businesses worked from the garage including a coach builder called Harry Barker. In 1935 Barker set up a business with his sons here. During the Second World War a bomb fell on the garage creating a mess in the form of a sea of black oil, but luckily there were no casualties.

128 Victoria Street – 1974

A portion of Victoria Street near to its junction with William Street during demolition in 1974.

129 The Royal Windsor Infirmary, Victoria Street

The Royal Windsor Dispensary and Infirmary was built in 1833-4 to replace the smaller premises in Church Street founded in 1818. In 1857, following a legacy, the building was extended and improved and in 1873 the adjoining Savings Bank was incorporated to provide two convalescent wards. By the end of the century it was realised that the building was too small and the governors decided to build a new hospital which became King Edward VII Hospital. This splendid Infirmary building was demolished in 1973.

130 The British School, Victoria Street – Preparatory Sketch c.1839

In May 1841 a new school opened in Victoria Street, opposite Victoria Barracks. This was known as the New British School and was built on land given by philanthropist Joseph Charriott. It could accommodate 180 boys and 120 girls. The school's first Headmaster was Joseph Lundy who remained Headmaster until 1860, when he opened his own private school in Kings Road. In 1871 the school was so popular that it had become over-subscribed; there were 215 boys, 117 girls and 103 infants. During the early twentieth century the numbers of children attending started to decline and it closed in 1930 and became the Windsor Education Office; it was demolished in the 1970s.

131 Fire and Police Station St Leonard's Road – 1907

The foundation stone for a new Fire Station and Police Station was laid in 1905 by Windsor's Mayor William Shipley. The building was constructed by Young James Lovell of Marlow, and took a year to build at a cost of £20,000. The Fire Station and Police Station were opened on the 30 October 1906 by Prince Christian, the High Steward of Windsor. In 1966 the fire station moved to new premises in St Marks Road and part of the building was converted into a venue for the arts in 1981. *See Colour Plate 23.*

132 Harrison's Cycle Shop in St Leonard's Road – 1955

Harrison's cycle shop was originally known as Elder's Cycle Store. In 1911 Ernest Harrison, who owned a newsagent's shop at 155 St Leonard's Road, purchased the cycle shop together with its stock for ten pounds. The business flourished but closed in the 1970s.

133 First Life Guards Church Parade, Holy Trinity Church – 1906

Church Parades to Holy Trinity Church by the 1st and 2nd Lifeguards were a popular sight in Windsor and they were often caught on camera. In this view the 1st Lifeguards parade outside Holy Trinity Church.

134 2nd Life Guards march past the Police Station from Trinity Church during WWI

Cavalry soldiers of the 2nd Lifeguards departing to the battlefields of the Great War outside the Police and Fire Station in 1915. The grim fact was that not many were to return.

135 The Opening of King Edward VII Hospital – 1909

The commemoration stone of the new hospital was laid by King Edward VII on the 22 June 1908. The King was accompanied by Queen Alexandra and their daughter Princess Victoria. In March 1909 the first patients were transferred from the Old Infirmary in Victoria Street, to the pristine facilities that the new hospital offered. It was designed by the architect A. William West. Most of the services originally offered by this hospital have now been transferred to Wexham Park, but there is an Eye Hospital in the building.

136 Entrance to Combermere Barracks, St Leonard's Road, c.1916

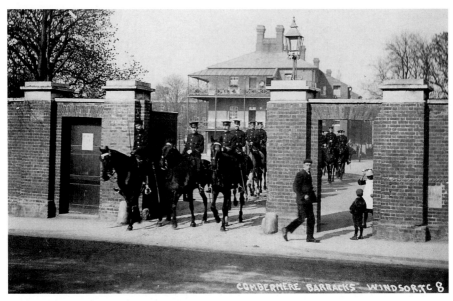

Troop of soldiers leaving Combermere Barracks by the old gate to exercise the horses. 'K' Block is seen in the background.

137 Lifeguards on Parade, Combermere Barracks – 1916

Life Guards' band on parade in Combermere Barracks. 'K' Block is in the foreground, and the Officers' Mess is seen in the distance.

138 Combermere Barracks c.1900

The band of the Household Cavalry playing on the lawn after church parade on a Sunday morning c.1900. The people of Windsor were invited to come and listen to the band. The Officers' Mess is seen in the background.

139 Combermere Barracks Parade Ground c.1916

The Combermere Barracks were built between 1800 and 1804 on a twenty acre site. This photograph shows 'K' Block which faced onto the parade ground. The balconies were added to the barrack block after a visit by Queen Victoria in 1868. The ground floor of the barracks was used as stables. In 1820 two hospitals were added to the barracks; one for the infantry and one for the cavalry. Queen Victoria visited the barracks in 1868, and in 1869 the barracks were refurbished. They were updated in the 1960s and again in 1970. The barracks were partly rebuilt and refurbished between 2004 and 2006.

140 The Kipling Memorial Building, Alma Road c.1970

The Kipling Memorial Building is named after Rudyard Kipling who attended the United Services College in 1878 in Devon. The United Services College moved to Windsor in 1906 and amalgamated with St Mark's School. In 1911 the school was renamed the Imperial Service College. Kipling Memorial Building was constructed in 1939 to provide much-needed accommodation for Connaught and Roberts Houses attached to the College. Benno Elkan was commissioned to create a plaque, see right, based on characters from Kipling's 'Jungle Book'. The plaque was erected on the south side of the building.

Due to financial restraints the school moved to Hertfordshire in 1942 and Kipling Building was sold to Windsor Corporation in 1943. By 1950 all the municipal departments which had previously been scattered throughout the town had moved into Kipling Building, which remained their home for the next twenty years. With the formation of the Royal Borough of Windsor and Maidenhead in 1974 many of the departments moved to offices in Maidenhead Town Hall. Kipling Building was now surplus to requirements and was sold to the Rank Hovis McDougall Company in 1981. It was demolished in 1982.

Benno Elkan's Lead Plaque based on characters from 'The Jungle Book'.

See Colour Plate 24.

Index